UNDERSTANDING *Your 8 year old*

UNDERSTANDING

Your 8 year old

Lisa Miller

of

THE TAVISTOCK CLINIC

Series Editor: Elsie Osborne

ROSENDALE PRESS

First published in Great Britain in 1993 by:
Rosendale Press Ltd
Premier House, 10 Greycoat Place
London SW1P 1SB

Design by Pep Reiff
Production Edward Allhusen
Typeset by Ace Filmsetting Ltd
Printed in the United Kingdom by Redwood Books

British Library Cataloguing in Publication Data
A catalogue record for this book is available from The British Library

ISBN 1 872803 45 8

The Tavistock Clinic, London, was founded in 1920, in order to meet the needs of people whose lives had been disrupted by the First World War. Today, it is still committed to understanding people's needs though, of course, times and people have changed. Now, as well as working with adults and adolescents, the Tavistock Clinic has a large department for children and families. This offers help to parents who are finding the challenging task of bringing up their children daunting and has, therefore, a wide experience of children of all ages. It is firmly committed to early intervention in the inevitable problems that arise as children grow up, and to the view that if difficulties are caught early enough, parents are the best people to help their children with them.

Professional Staff of the Clinic were, therefore, pleased to be able to contribute to this series of books to describe the ordinary development of children, to help in spotting the growing pains and to provide ways that parents might think about their children's growth.

THE AUTHOR

Lisa Miller worked as a teacher after leaving university at Oxford. She trained as a child psycho-therapist at the Tavistock Clinic, London, where she now works in the Department of Children and Families. Her time is divided between clinical work and teaching; and she is responsible for the Under-Fives Counselling Service which offers up to five interviews for any parent or parent-to-be concerned about a baby or small child.

Her publications include editorship (with Margaret Rustin, Michael Rustin and Judy Shuttleworth) of "Closely observed infants": an account of the method of infant observation pioneered at the Tavistock.

Lisa Miller is married with four children.

CONTENTS

INTRODUCTION

"Give me a child until he is seven, and then anyone can have him," said Ignatius Loyola. And while you can argue about the extent to which this is true – after all, a lot of development takes place after the eighth year – there is still something which we tend to accept nowadays in the idea that the basic lines of somebody's character are laid by the time they are eight. Undeveloped patches can expand and flourish, unsuspected strengths can appear. Conversely, hidden difficulties can emerge; and one always has to allow for the effect of experiences, good and bad, which contribute to growth or which disturb and damage. But during the intensity of the earliest years, in their rapid development, a child has become recognisably the person he or she will be for life.

A glance at what is or has been expected of an eight year

old gives us some idea of where the child of this age stands in the human life-span. In Great Britain, for example, our children move from the Infant School to the Junior School at this age. This move is quite in harmony with the child's development psychologically, socially and intellectually. He or she is moving out of the more intimate world of the closer family and the educational approach based loosely on a family model. Now something more of independence is asked of the boy or girl in the Junior School. The slightly tougher world he or she enters is not merely imposed by society from outside; it is in tune with the point in a child's growth where he or she casts off and begins to travel more independently.

One could collect examples, past and present, which testify to this feeling that a decisive move is made in the eighth year, that the first seven years are devoted to taking in fundamental necessities for psychological survival and that after this some degree of independence from parents and home is feasible. We may remember that in the Middle Ages small boys destined to be knights left their parents to be pages in some other household at about this age. They moved on again to become squires at the age of about fourteen, and there seems to be a consensus that there is something particular about these middle years of childhood, between the first seven or eight years on one hand and puberty on the other.

Perhaps it is as well to stress that there is much variation between children, that eight year olds differ greatly from each other, that individual children reach different stages at different times. However, I hope that enough generalisation is possible to make a book like this interesting for those of us who are concerned with eight year olds. Belinda, who was devoted to her dolls, begged for what she called "a last doll" for her eighth birthday. Robin, keen on cricket, wanted a "proper bat". This didn't mean that Belinda absolutely gave up her dolls, any more than it meant that Robin's game was transformed into something highly polished. Both of them, though, happened to have had a feeling about their eighth birthday. It would be no good looking out for it in every child; you would certainly find that many eighth birthdays pass without any comparable feeling. Belinda, and Robin, however, were both as individuals in touch with a feeling of good-bye to early childhood which is in the air at this stage of life.

CHAPTER ONE

YOUR DEVELOPING EIGHT YEAR OLD

What stage have we reached?

I have just commented on the child's good-bye to the early years. This is a gradual thing. During the Infant School years – five to seven - an important emotional change comes over the child. Pre-school children are whole-heartedly engaged in family relationships: mummies and daddies and babies preoccupy them. They are prey to strong feelings, to bad dreams and passing fears of giants or witches or monsters. Both boys and girls go through periods of being fiercely attached to mum or to dad and wishing the other parent (or other grown ups) out of the way. There is intense interest in new baby brothers and sisters – their own or other people's – and all sorts of jealousies and envies as well as passionate attachments appear. This tends to quieten down after the age of about five and, by the age of eight, children are well established in a different emotional atmosphere.

Emily was three when Sam was born. A family friend knew them well and saw a lot of them. He went abroad while Sam was about two and did not see them again until Emily was nine and Sam five. Of course he expected vast changes to have happened, but the nature of these changes intrigued him. Before he left, he had watched Emily change from the "perfect little mother" she wanted to be when Sam was born into rather a cross, rivalrous little girl who couldn't sustain an imitation of the mother she started out with; she went through a rough patch when it was clear that she was furious with everyone; with her parents for having a baby without consulting her, with Sam for being born and for being so adorable, with her mother for being big and able to have babies, with her father for preferring to be married to mummy rather than devoting all his attention to Emily. This was one side. The other side was a real interest in Sam and a real wish to be like her parents and to learn to help with Sam. There was also a genuine affection for the baby, pleasure in his development and delight in the fact that he so clearly admired her. However, the atmosphere in the house inclined to be tempestuous. Both parents were often very tired: Sam would wake to be fed; Emily would have bad dreams. Should they struggle to keep them in their own beds? How could the parents cope with this jealousy? They felt sorry for Emily, taken aback when their elder charming child showed a different side to her nature; but they were also aware of needing to protect Sam.

And frequently they disagreed. Tiredness softened them up and, like Sam and Emily, they quarrelled. The family friend, childless himself, was rather astonished at the nature of the passions unleashed.

When he came back he found a different family. Not only Emily but all the family seemed somehow to have moved into calmer waters. Family expeditions, communal interests, seemed more possible: the family could go off as a group to theme parks or swimming pools. The children's parents were good tennis players and first Emily, now Sam, had been issued with a racquet. Their parents were happy to pick up this interest again. Emily had lots of activities – she played the piano and went to Brownies. Sam longed to do similar things. It was noticeable that the relationship between Sam and Emily had changed. It was quieter. Sometimes they played together with great pleasure. On other occasions you could see that they had settled for a kind of truce. Emily had identified herself as big sister with a teacherly sort of person. "Sam, hold my hand. *Never* step off the pavement!" or, "Oh Sam, that's lovely! What a clever drawing!" and "Did you know, Sam's learning to *read*!" Emily, if the truth be told, was a bit condescending. However, Sam remained uncrushed. Sometimes you would still see the young child in him – the bit that was three or four, not even five. He fell into tantrums, howling rages even with his admired Emily: he had a funny habit of trying desperately hard to be rude and bellowing things like, "You raspberry! You rose-tree! You fish-cake!" Emily was embarrassed at this. She regarded all things babyish as rather silly, and threw all her energies behind urging the far-from-reluctant Sam to be a proper schoolboy.

The whole atmosphere of the family had altered on his return. In this case the mother had taken up a full-time job again and the feeling was that the white-heat of the nursery had gone. There are many ways of looking at this change of mood. One interesting one was formulated by Freud in the first place; he drew our attention to the way in which small children are deeply involved in the most important facts of life. Children between babyhood and school age are taken up with enquiries about where they come from, with questions about the difference between grown-ups and children, about the relationships between adults, with matters of love and hate, God and death. Then a different period of emotional development ensues. Between the turbulent earliest years and the first stirrings of puberty – probably around the time of transfer to secondary education at eleven in this country – comes a patch of time, where children feel the need to put something of a damper on their more ardent feelings, to develop interests beyond the family and family relationships.

The small boy who at four said about his nursery-class teacher, "I think I'll *marry* Miss Edwards when I grow up," would be pretty horrified at eight at the bare idea of anyone, let alone himself, taking Ms Thomas, his present teacher, to the altar. The little girl who unselfconsciously called her dolls her babies and dressed up as mummy at playgroup may or may not still be interested in these things but she will almost certainly have lost that uninhibited, sometimes dramatic wish to experiment with being a grown-up in play. Children have entered into the stage where they are marking time, waiting to be grown-up. The human animal takes a long time to arrive at maturity. There is a lot to be done and much to be enjoyed in these Primary School years; and they have a flavour of their own.

Our eight year old is in the full fling of this time. How can we characterise it further? Before I go more systematically into the needs and wishes of the eight year old I should like to try to describe this particular flavour more carefully. What is the typical eight year old like?

Keeping the rules

Eight year olds have generally cottoned on to the fundamental differences between acceptable and unacceptable, nice and nasty, good and bad, right and wrong. On the whole this is not a time of life when they want to have their prejudices and beliefs challenged. That will come later: indeed, children of this age can be cheerfully and enthusiastically smug. They like good causes – "Save the Whales", "Save the Rain Forests" – where you can be vigorously and uncomplicatedly on the side of right.

Dan's friend Harry went to Cubs. Dan asked if he could go too. His mother hesitated. She had always thought that Cub Scouts were a bit questionable – old-fashioned, rather rigid, looking back to Rudyard Kipling and the days of the Empire; surely there was something more flexible and up-to-date? But she felt she couldn't keep Dan from trying it out and decided to keep a sharp eye on things for signs of political incorrectness. She was taken aback by how from the very start Dan loved Cubs. It seemed to answer to something in him: he liked the ceremonies, the organised games; he thrilled to the idea of going to camps; he chatted away about Baden-Powell and the history of the Scout movement and as time went on he amassed a formidable array of badges for all sorts of bits of expertise, like cooking and swimming, first aid and music.

Dan's mother realised gradually that Cubs were not only a pleasure but quite a relief for Dan. She was a single mother, very close to Dan who was her main companion. While she had protected him as much as she could from her major adult worries, she had no grown-ups living with them to whom she could turn. So naturally Dan had been close up against an adult mind – his mother's – which had been full of all sorts of anxieties, including ones about Dan's upbringing. Was she too strict? Too lax? Ought she to encourage this? Should she be worrying about that? For Dan the Tuesday evenings at Cubs were like a version of some of the things he already valued about school, though Cubs could be simpler and more straightforward.

I shall talk later about the *content* of an eight year old's interest and think more then about what Dan liked doing with the Cubs. Just here we are thinking about the eight year old's appreciation of clear guide-lines, and a feeling that on the whole the grown-up world is formed of people who are in agreement about what is right and what is wrong. At Cubs good behaviour was pretty clearly defined for Dan and his fellows. It meant throwing yourself into the activities provided, keeping the rules of the games, experiencing the safety of the group. Helpful behaviour was praised and underlined; gardening, First Aid, things like that. What's more, you weren't left with time on your hands to get into mischief. This didn't mean that all the boys at Cubs were beautifully behaved – far from it. But there was little doubt about what you should and shouldn't do, and there was a reassuring feeling that Akela (the leader of the pack) and his helpers were in control and in agreement.

Dan may have specially enjoyed this because he had to take a good deal of responsibility at home. He was aware that there was no-one to help his mother and that she was often exercised by complicated worries. But many eight year olds hanker after similar experiences in one form or another, whether at school, in the family, in books or on television. This is a time of life where they are stepping out to a new degree of independence and where they also need firm backing and support. Another thing that Dan responded to at Cubs was the repetition, the regularity, the little rituals. All this formed a framework within which he could enjoy himself. Eight year olds need boundaries, as all children and young people do; they need clear and predictable ones because this is a stage of consolidation. At a pre-school age they were preoccupied in an emotional way with discovering the big differences between love and hate, right and wrong. At this age the preliminary groundwork has been done. But in these pre-adolescent years the child is not yet strong enough to wrestle with too much in the way of moral conflict. Individual children may be thinking hard to themselves, with their friends or teachers or parents. For instance, Dan enjoyed his "Health Education" discussions at school where his lively young teacher chatted with the class about the rights and wrongs of things like how you behave with your friends. But he needed to feel that the grown up world around him was reasonably solid.

It can be a difficult matter to judge how much responsibility an eight year old can assume for himself or herself. It is as well to remember that he or she is still dependent on rules. I am thinking here about the sort of rules you can cling to, just as much as the deeply ingrained, deeply understood ones which become part of ourselves. The eight year old Emily, telling her small brother Sam about how to cross the road, obviously relished the rules she had been taught. "At the kerb, stop, look and listen!" she declared. "Look right, look left, look right again. If there's nothing coming, quick march straight across!" Her mother listened, rather amused and even sheepish, because when she heard Emily reciting this, she realised these were words *she* had been taught twenty-five years before. She had clung on to them, remembered them – and only half aware had made

Emily memorise them too. While she and Emily were both more sophisticatedly aware of the need to think while crossing the road, Emily also had her rule to fall back on if need be.

Relationships: adults and children

Girls and boys of this age are still dependent on grown-ups psychologically just as much as physically and practically. However, they tend to be less interested than in earlier years in the parents as a couple, and as a baby-producing couple. Many parents have had the experience of telling a tiny child that a new baby is on the way and having the news greeted by a curious lack of surprise.

This reminds us that tiny children have a tremendous preoccupation with new babies and seem half to be expecting them all the time, even when they don't materialise. The eight year old has pushed such preoccupations to the back of the mind. Sex and sexuality do not loom large. Children of this age have some years to wait until puberty, adolescence and finally sexual maturity, and it is as though they want not to have to think about these things too much.

I can imagine some mothers and fathers laughing and thinking, "What on earth is this woman talking about? There's nothing like a primary school playground for dirty jokes!" It certainly is true that there is a strong streak of lavatorial humour running through the awareness of children at about this age. And the jokes they make about sex are almost like lavatory jokes; it isn't for nothing that they're called "filthy". The point seems to be that they tend to think about sex – when they do – in denigrating fashion. It's as though they are temporarily out of touch with sexuality as linked with love, hate and knowledge and out of touch with the grand passions. Yet it does them no good to make too many dirty jokes. These may cause paroxysms of giggles and a feeling that the jokes have successfully defied the silly grown ups' rules. But soon they will start feeling uncomfortable about it, if it is allowed to continue unchallenged, especially unchallenged in full view and hearing of the adults.

The child of this age seems to feel most comfortable with parents and adults who keep fairly clearly to a well-defined adult role. It may seem exciting if a grown up joins in the "pee, pooh, belly, bum, knickers" kind of joke, but only for a short while. In the same way, children like to keep the blinds drawn on real adult sexual activity. At the present time we are in a state of questioning and some confusion: we do not want to be tight-lipped and prudish, banishing all mention of these matters, especially at a time when sex education seems so vital in relation to AIDS. At the same time it is clear that a child in these middle years of childhood is not happy if he or she is not allowed to place these matters on something of an emotional back burner. A child like Margery, for example, whose parents had divorced and who had both formed new relationships, was disturbed not only by the breakdown of her parents' marriage but also by having their sexuality brought far too vividly to her notice. Her mother consulted a Child Psychotherapist who felt that Margery's disturbed nights, lack of progress at school, and general state of anxiety could be linked to the way in which she could not get to grips with the new state of affairs.

And a significant factor in her *not* being able to deal with her parents' new partners and the new pattern of her life was the fact that she could not stop herself mentally getting right into their sexual relationships. She used to investigate her mother's drawers, her father's girl-friend's bag. She needed the grown ups to place her outside their bedroom, both literally and metaphorically, and to remember that someone of eight cannot take on adult conflicts and adult emotions; all Margery felt was a horrible mixture of feeling excluded and lonely, with tantalising adult experiences just beyond her reach, and also of feeling over-excited and over-stimulated in a way which could lead nowhere.

We can take note of the interesting way in which the books children like at this age do not generally deal with adults much. Even those which address really important questions place adults at the perimeter, forming the essential background, holding the circle within which the action is played. Those of us who have read books like *Charlotte's Web* by E. B. White see how questions of universal human experience – love and change and loss, for example – can be written about from the child's point of view. We can see how the child of this age does have a child's eye view which must be respected.

Going even further there are many books where the adults have been positively dismissed from the scene, often before the story is under way. C. S. Lewis's *Chronicles of Narnia* take Peter and Susan, Edmund and Lucy into a world of their own. E. Nesbit's children in *The Wouldbegoods* or *The Phoenix and the Carpet* have absent parents and parents always take a back seat in Enid Blyton's criticised but popular stories. (I am not suggesting that your eight year old should be able to read these books to himself or herself, of course; some may but they will be the exceptions. However, many eight year olds will respond eagerly to the stories if they are read to them and come to read them a little later.) The point I am making is that these stories are in tune with the inner world of our eight year old – the inner world of the imagination of conscious and unconscious thinking, of the preoccupations characteristic of this stage of life. Here the grown-ups' world tends to be separate from the children's world, although in the stories themselves we see the children working away hard to prepare themselves for adult life, or to fill the time until they reach adulthood.

This reflects the growing importance of groups to children at this age; the importance of school, teams, classes, friends, gangs and the corresponding importance of the adults who run those who also need to hold the circle, acting often more like uncle, aunt or older sibling than like mum or dad.

Relationships: girls and boys

Just as children move away from their early intense interest in the mother-father couple, or people who represent couples of all types, so they move into a rather different relationship with each other. One way of looking at this age group is, as I said earlier, to regard it as an age where earlier findings are consolidated. One important discovery of the earliest years is the discovery that you are either a girl or a boy. At this later time energy is expended on re-inforcing and consolidating this discovery. There is a special way children have at this age of making sure that they are clear about the fact that girls are girls and boys are boys, particularly in reference to themselves. Before they can satisfactorily explore all the different aspects of their characters they need to be more or less safely grounded in their own identities.

Hence you get the decisive split that happens in most playgrounds a good deal of the time. Boys play with boys, girls with girls. This particular stage of development has sometimes been underlined by the practice of setting up separate schools for girls and boys. There are different opinions on this, but the fact remains that it is by no means impossible to educate the sexes separately, and the children themselves seem happy with it. But whether they are actually in separate schools or not, this seems the age when they like to spend some of their time with friends or groups of the same sex, feeling comfortably ensconced in their sameness, not wanting the challenge of difference at present. From this position, where Dan has an underlying confidence that he is a boy like Harry and Steve, and Emily has the safe knowledge she is a girl like Susie and Anne, each can make forays across boundaries and think what it is like to be someone else.

Susie lived next door to Harry and played with him all the time until they started gradually to draw apart from the age of about six. Their parents were rueful and hoped that the friendship could be maintained, but although Susie and Harry continued to chat in a companionable way to and from school, and to swap anecdotes about teachers or school work, their interests had temporarily divided and they chose to invite quite other friends round to play. However, their mothers naturally and reasonably hoped that this was not a permanent state and that Susie and Harry could draw together again later. It is tempting to try to combat what one thinks of as sexist behaviour, and certainly a rigid reinforcement of some imagined absolute difference between boys and girls can only lead to a hopeless feeling that the sexes are inaccessible to each other. But at this age children may tend to be sexist. After all, we must remember that this is what sexism *is* – an immature understanding of the nature of men and women and the relationship between them. So we should not be surprised if boys go around claiming that girls are soppy weeds, and girls that boys are rough and stupid, but just do our best to keep a different reality alive in an unobtrusive way.

There have always been plenty of activities where boys

and girls can and do join up in a friendly way. Virginia Woolf and Rupert Brooke played cricket together in Cornwall on holiday as children. Jane Austen's nineteenth century heroine Catherine Morland's favourite activity at this age was rolling down the green slope at the back of the house and playing baseball. Lots of girls now play football. Children cooperate happily on projects in the classroom. Those children who are best grounded in their own identity will be the ones who can be in touch with something boy-like *and* girl-like inside themselves. The cheerful, vigorous hearty little girl can be the one who may well agree with her friends that boys are a nuisance but who nevertheless can join in things with her brothers, read stories with boys in them, show a wide range of interests. Another look at children's literature will show examples of this sort of thing: for instance, the hero of Lynne Reid Banks's *The Indian in the Cupboard* is a thorough boy, but the whole story (which tells how a little toy Red Indian comes alive, and about what a problem it is to look after him) is about how concerned, protective, involved the young hero becomes and how his feelings are positively motherly.

More of a worry is the child who seems unhappy with what he or she is. Anthony, who was nine, only ever played with the girls. Plump, slow-moving and alternately boastful and shy, he looked rather like his mother. Putting himself with the girls seemed to be based on his fear of the boys. He was depressed, and a closer look at him in depth revealed a child from a family in difficulties where the father was physically ill but often also violent. It was as though he had despaired of ever growing up to be a man, and unfortunately, too, as though he had a sad picture of what it meant to be a woman.

Amy stuck exclusively with the boys. She wanted to wear boys' clothes – not just the sort of clothes which are attractively unisex and which are popular with this age-group. She wanted boys' underwear and boys' heavy shoes. You did not need to be a professional to think that Amy was not a happy girl. Any signs of a real rejection of your own sex are worrying: some questions needed to be asked about Amy, who was not what used to be called "a tomboy" but somebody who did not think it was safe to be a girl. She did not look like a girl who was finding satisfaction in exploring different sides to her nature; she was pale, anxious and truculent, and she was having a lot of difficulty in learning. She had never known her father, and her mother had died of cancer. We cannot tell from this exactly what pushed her to try to get inside the character of a boy or a man, but Amy needed professional help from someone who was able to give her the time, attention and expertise to come to an understanding of the anxieties leading to her fear of joining the other girls.

This opening chapter has tried to place the eight year old as the developing human being, the future woman or man at that stage of development when the original family is ceasing to be the central reference point. Before looking at the child in the family, let us look at the wider world of society which is opening up and which puts new demands on the child at this time.

CHAPTER TWO

AT WORK AND PLAY

School

There is no eight year old for whom school is not important. How he or she is managing matters a lot. It is at this stage – the transfer to Junior School, that teachers and parents are able to see what a child has made of the previous years in Nursery and Infant School and how well-equipped the previous experience has made him.

The earliest years of education (in the broadest sense) should, and generally do, take into account the fact that young children relate primarily to the adult, secondarily to the children. A good reception class infant teacher knows how much like a mother she has to be to her charges. She knows that children require a lot of supervision and that they are only just beginning to be able to get along without the feeling that they can at any time refer to a grown-up. Because *all* the children need this, and also because there is a wide range of capacity in children (some more ready for school at five than others) it is possible for a boy or girl to go right through the early years without much difficulty and yet run into heavy weather in the Junior School.

Two contrasting children of this sort were Terry and Adrian. Terry had arrived in Nursery class with an overdeveloped capacity to look after himself. At the age of four he had already developed quite an armour-plating of streetwise toughness in imitation of those elder brothers with whom he spent his time hanging around. He was pushful, boastful and constantly played at being Superman. However, the nursery class teacher was not deceived. She soon realised that inside this protective shell was a vulnerable, anxious Terry who felt he lived in a dangerous world and tended to lash out to get in his blow first or to resort to magical fantasies like Superman and pretend he was invincible. The teacher's sympathetic attention, her pointing out to the nursery assistants how fragile Terry really was, was extremely helpful. She did her best to stop Terry doing things he shouldn't. This went some way towards preventing him from building up a picture of himself as a bad, bold boy, a picture that neither he nor the staff and children would be able to ignore. Setting limits on his behaviour, stopping him hitting other children and snatching the toys, saved Terry from running up a bill of guilt he could not begin to pay. At the same time the teacher tried to look after the needy bit of him, the bit that hadn't been a baby long enough. However, although this approach could be managed while Terry was five and six, it grew harder as he came to be seven and eight. This was partly because he was a child who had never had enough attention in babyhood: his mother was struggling with bad housing, insufficient money, no moral support, too many boys and a background of deprivation herself. So although his teachers all had some understanding of the problem, it remained hard for Terry to develop and to learn. If he felt wobbly and unsure, he quickly became Superman; and as the demands on him became greater he felt more and more precarious.

Now, during the first and second years in Junior School, all the other children in the class could read properly, the slower ones had caught up, and it was clear as it never had been before, that Terry was really behind. He started to resort again to his hard outer self, his "don't care" pose, his character of wide-boy. He began stealing. When you look at it dispassionately, it doesn't seem so hard to imagine why Terry should steal. First of all, he probably heard a lot of bragging talk from his elder brothers who had gone ahead of him in deprivation and delinquency. It was a real option – to be anti-social. Secondly, and more important, Terry must have felt needy, empty, lacking in something; he tried to fill this emptiness by taking things. Thirdly, he knew that stealing would bring him to everyone's attention. You could see it as an action saying, "Look! See what I've got to do! How long before you pay me proper attention?" The problem with someone like Terry is that he often needs more than the school can give. In this case Terry was lucky; the school was able to give him considerable extra help and attention and to continue to be able to treat him as a special case, rather than just a naughty boy. He needed a combination of firm holding and individual care which simply is not possible in a large class without the additional "special needs" help which Terry's school was able to secure.

The second child, Adrian, whom I mentioned, was different. He was a charming child, the youngest of a sizeable family. He coasted through Infant School, just about learning to read and acquiring the elements of number work. Popular and easy-going, he was allowed to travel at his own pace, which was leisurely. Again, the very fact that children develop at varying speeds masked the way in which Adrian was failing to engage with certain aspects of school. "They're all just babies, really," said one teacher to another affectionately, looking at Adrian's class while they were infants. This was quite true, but some of the babies were purposefully making their way onwards, and Adrian was not. All through the Infant School and into the first year of the Juniors he continued to do little bits of work, scraps of drawing, parts of projects; he half-read books, half-wrote stories, half-learnt songs. At eight and a half he went up into the second Junior form and met Miss Smith.

Miss Smith prided herself on being able to judge when it was necessary to confront a child with the fact that he was not doing his best. She watched Adrian carefully; she thought she could detect an edge of contempt for her as he produced a charming smile and an excuse for lack of work. Soon the crunch came. Adrian noticed that Miss Smith was pretty brisk. He began to look nervous, to avoid her eye. Then she systematically began to show him that his work was really not up to scratch. He hadn't finished this, hadn't read that; his excuses were plainly fabricated – finally, Adrian went home, burst into tears, said he hated Miss Smith, couldn't do his lessons and wanted to leave school.

His parents, alarmed, arranged to see Miss Smith. However, even in the fortnight that had already passed, Adrian's work was improving. Miss Smith was able to discuss him with his mother and father and to show them that she thought Adrian really had some problems which could only be conquered if he was determined to do it. He had been evading his anxieties. It turned out from subsequent talks and from what his parents gathered from Adrian that he had been carrying something of a burden. Convinced he was no good at his work, he had been charming his way out of it. But this left him both with a feeling that he wasn't clever, wasn't capable – and also with a feeling that you could pull the wool over grown-ups' eyes. This in turn made him think uneasily that grown-ups weren't much good. Who would help him with his predicament? Miss Smith lightened his burden by conceding that it existed. Where other teachers, understandably, had let Adrian pass as a delightful child, a little slow perhaps, but imaginative and never a trouble, Miss Smith helped Adrian to stop denying that he had a bit of a problem.

This problem could be solved. It could be solved by Adrian's gritting his teeth and doing the work even when he didn't feel like it. Then, of course, he had something to show for his efforts, felt better, and became convinced he had some potential.

Now, this fearless approach, confrontational and challenging to Adrian's previous theories about how to manage in class, would not have done for Terry at all. Adrian was a child who had plenty of good experiences; he needed to be turned round and set on the right track and aided to use his own existing resources. Terry was much more fragile and lacking in these resources. Though Adrian became frightened and persecuted for a time, he got over it very well as he faced his fears of never being able to achieve and proved them wrong. Terry's fears were stronger and deeper and if Miss Smith had added to them by chasing him up and telling him sharply his work wasn't good enough, he would have become even more mutinous and aggressive.

Learning to work

In the last section we saw how Adrian and Terry were both at this stage identified as having difficulties with learning and working and how this is the stage in school that shows up such problems.

Of course, children work all their lives. The new-born baby's work is suckling and very hard work it can be too, judging by the intensity of effort some babies put in. It can be hard work learning to balance three bricks on one another, hard work to learn to walk. The three or four year old who perseveres in doing a jigsaw or who sticks at trying to play with a friend who's being awkward is certainly working. Too early emphasis on school as a place of work is harmful. The informality of good early education is a necessary ingredient and children acquire skills and knowledge without much awareness of the line between work and play.

However, by the time a child is eight some distinction is usually there. The question is: how can we try to keep alive the idea in them that work is satisfying, purposeful, enjoyable, just as mastering that jigsaw was? How can that be married with the undeniable fact that not *all* work is fun and that doggedness is as essential as spontaneous flair? At this age, of course, these considerations are only just beginning to enter parents' minds. This is as it should be. Grinding away at endless sheets of sums is a way of ensuring a hatred of maths forever: there are plenty of ways of putting a child off work.

But there is another way of looking at those sums. Do they have to be slavery? How can good will and ingenuity join forces to produce the idea that practising sums is acquiring a skill, a skill which will give satisfaction like any other?

This is a great age for acquiring skills, or it is at least the age at which the concept of doing so seems to come to the forefront of a child's mind. We only have to look at the repertoire of extra activities which children undertake to see this. They start to join football, judo, tennis, cricket, skating clubs and to go every week to play and practise. They take up musical instruments – notoriously needful of practice – or ballet dancing, tap dancing, gymnastics; they learn to ride horses or to swim and dive. We have to distinguish, of course, between the child's own wish to do any of these things and the parents' wish for him or her to do so.

It is not a bad idea if we examine our motives and think a little bit about what drives us to take our children along. Is it because we have a genuine interest that we long to hand on? Is it because we refused to play the piano in youth and have bitterly regretted it since? Do we long for our child to shine? Not to be left out? Having gone through this, though, it must be said that we are still left with the way in which all these things seem to suit the child in these middle years. First of all, they are physically and psychologically able to manage things they couldn't do before. They can make a start on things they couldn't have attempted two or three years ago. And all these things I have mentioned have one in-built advantage: if you find the right one for you and you put in a bit of effort, you are almost bound to gain facility.

With these sports and activities just as with writing poems and stories or performing in school plays a child gains psychologically from feeling that something good, nice, worth doing has been achieved. The child who takes part in

the class assembly, having worked hard to make it a success, or the child who brings home an exercise book full of work at the end of term is at an unconscious level feeling that things are able to be made all right. Here is the antidote, the repairing agent for putting right things that have gone wrong. The reparative drive is a force in our natures which needs full play. Children who are *not* helped to do their best are deprived of an important chance to feel they have made a worth-while contribution to school or home life: pleasing people, not slavishly but generously, is essential.

It is at this age that teachers and parents alike can start to see where a child's strengths are, and also where the weaknesses are and begin the delicate job of encouraging talents and plugging gaps. It isn't always easy. Rebecca started to learn the piano and proved to be very good indeed. Within a year or so of starting her teacher was saying she could be exceptionally good. Her parents realised that soon they could be faced with some choices that they thought they must consider well. Should she start a second instrument? The violin? Her teacher was keen on this. Perhaps they even ought to consider the possibility of Rebecca's going to a special music school. At this point they pulled themselves up short and remembered that she was only eight-and-a-half. Surely, they thought, to slant her life too acutely towards music at this age would be taking a decision for her which she ought to have more say in herself. It must be possible to continue her music, and to help her to work hard at it, without its being the most important thing in her life. Her mother, as the parents talked, recalled having been sorry for people on television like skaters and gymnasts whose training from earliest years had conditioned their lives. Her father added that there must be an awful lot of would-be professional pianists around. Unless Rebecca really wanted to do that of her own volition later on, he thought they should plump for a decent general education and keeping options open.

Rebecca's parents remembered how young eight is. Of course, even at that age children *can* take matters into their own hands. Rebecca's music teacher also taught another little girl the same age, called Kate. Kate's three older siblings were all musical: they were a good bit older and Kate's mother was looking forward to having the noise of piano practice starting up again. But Kate loathed it. It wasn't that she wasn't musical: she could sing in tune. Kate was made to struggle on; she even passed an exam rather well. All the time, however, it was her mother pushing her, and just before her ninth birthday Kate's mum decided sadly that enough was enough. Something had to come from Kate herself. Kate may well regret her decision in future years, but the well-known proverb holds good in these things: you can take a horse to water, but you cannot make him drink. It was a while before Kate developed musical interest of her own, but eventually she did, and her mother had wryly to acknowledge that some things you cannot force. Kate was not only being put further off music in general, but she was being given an opening into the undesirable idea that work is forced drudgery.

Games and sports

The previous section discussed some of these pastimes and activities with the emphasis on how an eight year old can start to enjoy acquiring a skill and putting some work into it. There are other aspects of such things which are also important.

When he was nearly eight Toby and a few other boys from his class started to go along to weekly cricket coaching lessons at a local leisure centre. They were lucky enough to have a bright, eager young Australian to coach them for that whole year, and the episode made an indelible mark on Toby.

This was for several reasons. Toby had been attracted by the idea in the first place because his father and grandfather had loved the game. It therefore had the meaning to him of identifying with two people he loved and admired. When he got there he found he could do it quite well, and his wish to emulate his father and grandfather made him enthusiastic. The coach, Jason, was pleased to find such a keen group of small boys. To Toby this was his first experience of being taught by someone who liked what he was teaching – a grown-up who was taking something really seriously. Toby had been taught by people who liked children and liked teaching but never by someone who seemed to be beckoning him on into a world which people didn't grow out of, a world peopled by heroes past and present.

Toby also relished playing in a team and playing by the rules: he began to have some understanding of what both these things meant. The team, as something you can be loyal to and do your best work for, can be an attractive and powerful influence on children of this age. Girls and boys equally warm to the feeling of unity and the sense that team-play and play by the rules is a way of harnessing competitive feelings and allowing them space, yet keeping them under control. This opens up as a possibility when children make the subtle move which distances them a little from their families and enables them to get into different sorts of groups like teams and classes.

The management of rivalry can be a useful thing. There are widely different views among parents on competition: the one extreme holds that children's competitive impulse (so evident in family life at times) should positively be sharpened. These people are all for ranking children in so called order of merit, perhaps in the old fashioned way with weekly lists of marks, or perhaps just with competition, tournaments, quizzes for sport, lessons and playtime alike. The other extreme is held by people who believe that children should never be compared with each other. Each is unique, each has merits and weaknesses; each should be regarded as an individual in his or her own right. This second viewpoint thinks the first is cruel; the first viewpoint thinks the second is sentimental. A middle position acknowledges that children are often competitive and tries to distinguish between a useful side to that impulse and a destructive one.

The useful side is related to our wish to do better and our wish to have a realistic picture of our own achievements and capacities. Every time a child thinks, "I can do better than that," there is a faint stirring of the urge which we call competitive. The question, "How well am I doing?" has also to be measured against some outside standard at sometime. In the end, no matter how desirable it may be just to improve upon our personal best, we still have to look up and see how it compares with other people's personal best if we are to use our talents and our work appropriately and where it is needed.

Thus to try to ignore all comparisons seems rather false, since children automatically compare people. At the same time, it is thoroughly dangerous to whet children's competitive urges to cut-throat level. This is where one begins to feel that comparisons are odious, when the only way of thinking about people's achievements is by ranking them. Children of this age tend to do this anyway; she's got twelve gold stars, he's got four; he's collected twenty-seven pictures of footballers, she's got five. To amplify this tendency pushes children in the direction of contempt for those whom they regard as further down the ladder, and towards the fantasy that when you beat people you simply annihilate, destroy, eliminate them. So not only do you instil undesirable feelings of contemptuous superiority, you also instil positive terror of losing, of being lower down and humiliated or wiped out.

So it is clear what a relief the notion of team competition and fair play all round can be. With rules to rely on and leaders to guide, children can play out rivalrous impulses without too many destructive fantasies. To return to Toby and his cricket: he found here a medium for pacing himself against other people; for improving his own skills, comparing them with what he did before; for working with a team and finding a place for all the players; for struggling with ideas about sometimes winning, sometimes losing, but always trying. Of course, Toby had only set the first foot on the ladder of all this at the age we are discussing. He had a long way to go.

It is at this age, however, that such ideas begin to have meaning. For the younger child, whose loyalties and rivalries are still only operating in a family mode, these ideas are not meaningful. But for the eight year old sport and games with rules now begin to make an impact. Board games begin to be popular, for much the same reasons as I have outlined above: you can practise managing the feelings that winning and losing give you. Many children at this age are simply not able to contain their rage and frustration at losing a game; whether it is one of pure chance like snakes and ladders or one involving some degree of skill, they find it a problem to master the fury which a contrary Fate inspires in them. It is all practice in knowing how to deal with your emotions when life says, "No."

And there are other elements in board games which are exactly in tune with the way in which children think at this age – totting up scores, getting ahead, seeing your opponent fall behind: these fit in with a quantitative view of the world rather than a qualitative one ("how many?" as opposed to "what sort?") and the hierarchical view of things, with a sort of ladder at the top of which sit the grandest cleverest people and at the bottom of which sit the smallest and least important.

Learning co-operatively

These ways of looking at the world are not the only ones employed, but they are strong at this age: we have to allow for them but not to over-cater for them. It is essential to make a broad space for work which is untouched by organised competitiveness. The best place for this space at eight years old is in the classroom. Good modern primary school teaching relies on co-operative endeavour and individual pacing and attention. It is one thing to be starting to enjoy the rules of team games like football, or to be having a nice time (or losing your temper) at Junior Scrabble or Lotto. Such attention to the competitive instincts is largely misplaced in the world of school learning.

All parents of children at this age know how exciting and rewarding it can be when a class project goes well. Susie and Harry were in the same class. Their teacher, Mrs Bridges, announced that the theme of their project this term was to be Ancient Egypt. You can imagine what this brought forth in terms of pyramids, hieroglyphics, pharaohs, mummies; in terms of the River Nile and its crops, in terms of ancient gods and goddesses. There was a wealth of art work; there was a visit up to London to the British Museum. In a project like this Mrs Bridges had perfected the art of getting work out of each child according to his or her ability, and offering help, instruction and advice according to his or her needs. Harry was particularly proud of an elaborate mask, which he could really tie on, of the Egyptian god Anubis. He was a slow writer, so Mrs Bridges contented herself with seeing that he was doing a balanced amount about each aspect of the subject, and noted that he was improving. Susie produced screeds of handwriting, dotted about with little drawings. Steve copied out an Egyptian recipe for baking bread and they all made little loaves. This tradition of active and adventurous, non-competitive learning was managed by Mrs Bridges who, at the same time, could be firm about the absolute necessity of perfecting your number skills. In all lessons she tried to give the children the reassurance that nobody was left out, that nobody's contribution was derided, that honest endeavour and talented flair both got recognition. This was her way of counter-balancing the children's tendency to grade themselves and each other. Her class regarded her with affection and respect as the generator of interest and the guardian of fair play – fair play in a deeper sense, probably, than the fair play ensured by the cricket coach.

Other interests

We can see that good schoolroom learning is full of interest and harmonises with the current state of affairs in the eight year old mind. What does appeal to this age-group, and why?

Dan and Harry agreed that the children's television programme "Blue Peter" had mysteriously improved. It hadn't, of course; they had grown into it. This programme and others like it caters for certain definite aspects of this sort of age-group. Here is a list of items which appeared on "Blue Peter" recently. There was an account of how a house being demolished had had a sort of "time capsule" buried in the foundations – a film made of happenings in 1927. We saw the first showing of this film – King George V and Queen Mary, the streets of London. There was a competition to find the best British sausages; there was a feature about environmentally friendly cars. Two lively young women presenters dressed up in plastic suiting and bathed a large hairy dog. Nigel Mansell, the World Champion Formula 1 racing driver, was interviewed. A group of children questioned the current Secretary of State for Education, about new plans in schools. The presenters got into gumboots and mudded out the "Blue Peter" garden pond for Spring.

Can we make any generalisations from this about what needs this sort of thing caters to? First of all, it is obvious that no matter how much larking around children like, they also unconsciously acknowledge the need for a solid diet of serious ideas. They often like facts. What were things *really* like in 1927? What does a World Champion *really* think? In controversy and argument, as I said much earlier, they feel safe with a secure moral framework: they take eagerly to ecologically sound ideas. The notion that the Education Minister is down-to-earth and prepared to talk sensibly to them appeals to that side of them which likes things to be explicable – once again, safe. Thrills and excitement or exploration often combine with fascinated trips into the past. Playfulness and practicality go hand in hand as the presenters struggle with a wet dog and incidentally give much accurate information about how, when, how often and where to bath a dog.

Children watch a lot of television. It is often a problem to limit this, partly because we as parents get ground down by repeated requests, partly because we feel relieved, if a bit guilty, when they're quietly occupied by it, partly because if they don't watch it at their own house they can go round to someone else's.

However, it does seem worthwhile to distinguish between useful television and the other sort. Television ranges from the positively thought-provoking (children's serials, story programmes, ones about the natural world, for instance) right through the cheerfully entertaining (cartoons, quizzes, features) to programmes which are rather rubbishy or which were never meant for children and are downright unsuitable. I think we may have to consider setting a limit to rubbish – and by that I mean to imply that some children use perfectly respectable and decent programmes as rubbish. Television can be used as an aid to mindlessness. It can be used to fill a gap so that you don't have to think. Looking back on this, it sounds moralistic, but this may be just what this age-group of children calls out in adults: they may *need* someone to say, "Enough's enough," and turn off the set. This is particularly true when it comes to programmes like some adult films, those where violence and sexuality may combine to over-stimulate and puzzle the child. Is this what being grown-up means? Is this what mum and dad are secretly like? Why do they stop us fighting and playing silly games if this is what they call adult? Even quite serious, non-violent adult programmes can be simply too much for an eight year old. He or she tries to cut off from some disturbing sights or thoughts automatically; but if they are forced upon him or her they do no good at all.

Steve saw the horror movie "Nightmare on Elm Street" at a friend's house in the company of the friend and some irresponsible elder brothers. It made a harrowing impression upon him and haunted his dreams for years. Eight year olds are working to keep fantasy and reality separate and well defined. They need to consolidate their awareness of the differences between fact and fiction, real and pretend, truth and lies. They have not been able to tell the difference reliably for very long yet. When these barriers are ruptured, when the world of dream and nightmare bursts into the room, eight year olds become frightened and perplexed, then confused and terrified. And there is no doubt but that they harbour a grudge against a grown-up world which fails to protect them.

Even when there is no question at all of this kind of

alarming viewing, it is quite salutary to sit down and watch television from time to time with our children and see what it is that they are taking in. Often we have nice surprises as well as unpleasant ones. Children at this age throw themselves into "soaps" of the harmless sort like "Neighbours" and sometimes have thoughtful, intelligent comments to make on life in Ramsey Street!

Imaginative games and toys

Eight is a great age for crazes and collections. A few years past it was "My Little Pony" for small girls and more recently we have seen "Teenage Mutant Hero Turtles" and plastic wrestling figures. We may feel impatient and rueful at the thought that toy manufacturers are manipulating our children's desires – and indeed, it seems a pity. But, financial outlay aside, there is precious little difference between collections of "Silvanian Families" (animals in dolls' houses) or Star Wars' figures, and collections of cheap picture cards or conkers which fall completely free from the tree.

These collections perform several functions. First, they bind you and your friends into a tight group. Second, rivalries can again be played out safely. Third, you can learn to exchange, swap, compare. Fourth, you can amass a great quantity of stuff and feel quite rich. Fifth, you can become an expert. It is surprising how scholarly, how careful eight year olds can be as they remember, list and arrange their collections. And then the toys or the objects you have collected can fulfil quite another need – they can also form the basis for imaginative play, either solitary or with friends.

Giles collected Lego bricks and with his younger brother Gary built skilful and complicated models. These models took different shapes, but often the game ended up shading off into being a game about battles. The fights were usually stylised and formal: the creations were not seriously damaged. Giles and Gary were good friends but the game acknowledged that earlier quarrels were still around. Partly they were being worked upon in the shape of these games, whose background stories, made up by the boys, were bloodthirsty. Partly a truce had been unconsciously agreed. The brothers had reached an age where they felt pretty much like one another: they could sink their differences and share interests. But, though their parents did not know it at the time, there were going to be more quarrels in the teenage years before they worked out a way of getting along.

Emma and Louise, best friends, collected rather pretty little dolls of a certain make. Both girls were good with their hands and a long-standing game started at this time. They concocted dresses and costumes of all sorts for the dolls, and arranged them in various tableaux. Sometimes the dolls would be in the garden, posing among the flowers in the rockery. Sometimes they would be arranged with dolls'-house furniture. A grandiose play of "Costumes Through the Ages" was planned and some little dresses were made, though the play was never completed or performed. The game, which also involved elaborate private story-telling about the various dolls who all had names and characters, had all sorts of meanings to it – one being related to the way in which all these beautiful dolls were got up in their best and arranged to look marvellous. It was as though they were in suspended animation. You might almost say that one function of these dolls was unconsciously to represent that aspect of Emma and Louise which was waiting to grow up, like sleeping beauties waiting to be awakened. Before anyone objects to this picture of Emma and Louise as a sexually stereotyped one, let me say that they were also active, athletic, little girls in jeans and jerseys.

CHAPTER THREE

YOUR EIGHT YEAR OLD'S EMOTIONAL WORLD

If any of you have come across the first book in this series, about babies, you may remember that babies' needs were described as falling into three categories: the need to be fed, the need to be held and the need to be cleaned up. In complex and far-reaching ways we continue to have these basic needs. And how do those fit in with another way of describing what is essential for our growth and good mental health - our need for human relationships, inside and out of the family?

Taking things in

All day long, at home, at school, everywhere, your eight year old is taking things in. Some of the things that are taken in are completely assimilated: they become part and parcel of the child's character and make-up for ever more. This is the way in which deep identifications are formed: certain things about a child's father or mother are absorbed into the child's inner world. It is an active process; a child is not a blank sheet for parents to inscribe upon; he plays his own part too. There is a combination at work: things that happen to a child combine with the reaction to it, with what he or she makes of it. Early figures do, of course, have a powerful effect, but they are taken in and digested, processed before they start to live in the child's mind: in short, as Walter de la Mare put it,

"Whatever Miss T eats
Turns into Miss T,"

but we have to allow for Miss T's powers of digestion as well.

There is little doubt but that eight year olds are both receptive and vulnerable still. They are receptive to good experiences and vulnerable to bad ones. Dinah's parents got divorced when she was eight. The divorce was an acrimonious one, but the couple did their best to conceal their mutual distrust and bitterness from Dinah and tried to come to arrangements over access visits and other arrangements which were firm and fair. However, disagreement and recrimination kept breaking through: Dinah's mother felt burdened at times by having all the basic care and Dinah's father felt resentful at only seeing her once a fortnight. The mother felt the father was irresponsible and the father felt the mother was carping, resentful and glum. Both parents, however, were extremely nice to Dinah. But unfortunately this did not mean that Dinah noticed only the niceness that was being directed at her. She dared not mention her anxieties about the smouldering rage she sensed between her parents; and, indeed, she was only partly aware that she noticed it and that it worried her. It became clear that something was wrong when her school contacted her mother and said that Dinah's work had gone seriously downhill – would her parents like her to see an educational psychologist? Dinah went along for a couple of appointments and the educational psychologist, Ms Highnett, proved to be not only interested in tests which established Dinah's potential and her level of achievement, but also in her state of mind and how she was feeling. In her feedback meeting with Dinah's parents she asked them to come both at the same time, in order to address those aspects of them which genuinely cared for Dinah and wanted to parent her. Ms Highnett described Dinah as a little girl of good ability who was nevertheless at present hampered by her fears and worries. In the stories she made up, the pictures she did, the way she performed in the tests, Ms Highnett could see that Dinah was feeling that she had to please and soothe everyone. Any coming-together of people was felt to be a potential row. Dinah was alarmed by angry feelings, and not just by angry ones – but *any* strong feelings. A story that might contain a hint of jealousy frightened her, as did a story with a scolding in it. One can easily see that Dinah could have lost her energy, her enterprise and her wish to grapple with problems: she felt suspicious of vigour and determination, as though they might easily turn bad, and the only path she felt able to follow was the one of least resistance. From this we see that experiences go into a child whether you want them to or not. Once

Dinah's parents stopped denying that she was hurt and worried, they were far more able to co-operate to help her and to master some of their mutual anger.

There is some comfort in the notion that things go in whether you mean them to or not; since all the *good* sides of family life – the times when people are patient and humorous, helpful and affectionate – have the chance of being assimilated just as much as more problematical experiences.

Good experiences remain in the very bones of our psychological make-up. Toby, the young cricketer who loved and admired and wanted to emulate his father, had absorbed some of his father's qualities without trying: he had taken in something of the father's good-natured determination and intelligence. This is very different from copying or imitating. Of course, Toby did at times do both these things. You could see him unconsciously imitate his father: one day at the seaside his mother nudged his aunt and said, "Look at those two! Aren't they alike?" Toby and his father were walking along the sands. They strode purposefully, turning their toes out slightly, both clasping their hands behind their backs. Toby looked just like a miniature version of his dad. It was as though he had stepped into his father's shoes. Or at times he would copy his father quite consciously: he would look to see how his father did something and do it likewise. But these resemblances are transitory; Toby can easily stop turning out his toes and give up copying dad if he doesn't feel like it any more. Really learned characteristics cannot be laid aside or forgotten. Toby learnt about being determined from his father and his father's approach to family life, from the parents' joint attitude towards Toby. Toby could no more lose or forget this than he could forget how to walk.

All sorts of learning – the conscious and the unconscious – are best undertaken in a happy co-operative atmosphere; and there are plenty of things which cannot be learnt if like Dinah you are pre-occupied and anxious. In the school setting, difficulties in learning always need to be looked at in the context of a child's life in general: we have to take into account their emotional state, which often is one (as with Terry, the deprived boy) that precludes taking things in. Dinah felt she daren't take anything in; Terry felt all that he could manage to do was steal.

Here is another boy, Barney, who had a problem in learning – and not just with lessons. His problem was with learning about relationships. At this age things which were not regarded as particularly worrying in a small child emerge as problems when they linger on in a child of whom more is expected. Barney, who had two elder brothers, was bossy and tyrannical. It was as if he had continued to occupy the central position that a baby has in the family long past the time he had outgrown it. At school he tried to hog the teacher's attention, and interrupted conversations or other children's contribution in a maddening way. He had grown larger but not grown *up*. Everyone expects a small child not to be able to share much, not to be able to take turns. This had continued in

Barney for too long, and now if he merely got his fair share he felt grossly deprived. If people didn't answer him at once he felt neglected. At the same time, he was spoiling things for others – he was far from well liked and far from happy.

He was not learning how to get on with other people, and he wasn't learning school lessons well either. His teacher noticed a funny thing about him. If you told him something – that tortoises hibernate, that three fours are twelve – he would very often answer, "I know." Sometimes he did know, sometimes he didn't. But always he seemed to feel it was shaming, silly or disgraceful not to know. He couldn't take up the position of seeker for knowledge. He couldn't think like a person who feels hungry for information or thirsty to hear a bit more of that exciting story. In short, he couldn't bear to feel that someone else, not he, had something good to offer; and he couldn't bear to feel like the dependent one in a relationship.

For Barney this was complicated. Apparently he was ruling the roost, but deep down he felt shaky and mistrustful. All the time he was yelling, "Give me that! I know that! I want that! My turn!" he wasn't really getting anything much. What he did get he felt he had bullied out of people.

Barney's parents sought professional advice and during a series of meetings of the whole family – mother and father, two elder brothers and Barney – with a child psychiatrist, it was apparent that Barney was allowed by all the others to behave like an indulged greedy baby, and also like a baby whose tantrums are positively feared. As the meetings progressed, it became clear that not only did the older boys feel exasperation and resentment about the family situation, but also that they had some perfectly sensible ideas about how things might be improved. They – and Barney too, in a way – wished that matters could be more under control. Slowly and with a lot of emotional effort, the *whole* family, including Barney, began to shift and alter. The parents, accustomed to giving way to Barney, began to join forces and limit his demands. Barney began to find it more comfortable and safer to take up his place as youngest. He began to hope he really could grow up to be like his brothers and to give up the fear that he was doomed to be a stupid baby (for this is how he used to see babies) for life. His brothers, finding him wanting to join in sensibly, were relieved and began to accept him as one of them. Barney had started to learn, but not till the whole family had done some thinking and learning and changing.

Security and trust

Much that has already been said illustrates the eight year old's need for a firm and reliable framework to his or her life. As with Barney, so with all eight year olds: the family is still central to their needs no matter how eagerly they may be sallying forth to a wider world. No eight year old can be considered apart from his or her family, and that is why the child psychiatrist who dealt with Barney decided to start by seeing the whole lot of them. What functions does a family perform for a child this age?

It performs important functions linked with all the questions of relationship-forming and emotional growth touched on earlier. It is the setting and the framework of your child's life. It plays a part in holding things together for the child, providing continuity, reliability, regularity, though perhaps it should be said that even a family that is not functioning well or has ceased to function can still be of vital significance in a child's life.

For most ordinary children there is the comforting and unchallenged assumption that their families are not going to go away. Things are probably least complicated for an eight year old when development can proceed within a reliable setting where holidays follow terms, lunch follows breakfast and new, different things (delightful, painful, challenging) are tackled within the context of the familiar. A child's past is contained in the family's memory; the parents' capacity to remember, to bear the child in mind, worry about him or her, puzzle away at problems, fight on a child's behalf – all these things which are taken for granted as part of parenting form a kind of container for the child's still immature self, a container which will often be symbolised by the family home. "I remember, I remember, the house where I was born," wrote Thomas Hood, and places take on lasting significance for a child.

It must not be thought that when I talk about a family I am only thinking of a family where the child lives with two parents and maybe brothers and sisters. It has to be recognised that family security can be provided in a lot of different ways: a family can mean a large extended family of grand-parents, or aunts and uncles all living closely together; it can mean one parent and one child; it can mean children adopted or fostered; it can mean a family separated by divorce or bereavement or re-constituted by second marriages or partnerships. All these are workable possibilities. It has to be said, however, that large changes and losses are hard for a child to accommodate, and we do a child no service if we deny this and say that they are fine when they aren't, and we shall think about this in a while. The essential ingredient of a family from a child's point of view is the way in which they go on being your family whatever happens. They are the furniture of your life, as well as being the objects of your deepest passions.

What other things give eight year olds a sense of security? School is very important. School, no matter how much you dislike it sometimes, is the place where you *ought* to be, the place where you've *got* to be, and in an odd way this gives you a feeling of being wanted. Your class-mates and friends give you a sense of who you are. Most schools understand the need for a rhythm to the school day, week and year; there is variety, of course, with some schools running a much more flexible timetable than others, but on the whole some pattern like "register, assembly, work, play, work, dinner, play, work, home" gives a comfortable, predictable rhythm to school life. Nobody would recommend a tight routine which takes away all spontaneity – all need for thinking about the unforeseen – but eight year olds value order and shape, partly because they are not yet old enough to construct and maintain their own. They need help and support.

This they get from the people who focus on them, at home and at school. Help and support are positively strengthening. It is the combination of in-put and back-up which enables growth. How do we strengthen an eight year old?

First of all, and most delightfully, we strengthen any child by focusing on him with appreciation, affection and praise for his endeavours. This is not usually too hard. Dan's achievements at Cubs pleased *him* so much that his mother had only happiness from saying how lovely his cooking was, how clever his First Aid achievements. It is a subtle matter, though. On the one hand, all children need somebody who at times is uncritically fond. Sometimes grandparents take up this favouring position; but, whoever it comes from, a child at times needs the feeling that there is someone who always prefers to see him or her as a swan rather than a goose. On the other hand, too much of this, too uncritical an appraisal, leads a child to suspect our sincerity or our brains! Terry at one point had a young support teacher who fell into ecstasies when Terry produced the slightest effort, thinking that undiluted encouragement was the way forward. Terry felt cynical about this, sensing the placating quality in it (the teacher was indeed nervous of Terry's truculence) and being able to tell for himself when he had put real effort into something and when he hadn't.

This leads us to a more general point. Just as Terry's teacher felt that he had to please Terry with his comments, so some adults feel that children *should* have nice experiences all the time, and that something has gone wrong when children have nasty experiences. If we step back, we can see rationally that the human condition dictates that we have a mixture of nice and nasty: as Blake says, "joy and woe are woven fine". There is no avoiding difficulty and anxiety, and the best we can do for our children is often to keep them company while they are miserable or in pain. I shall return to this, to treat it from a slightly different angle. Here I want to think about support in difficulty, helping an eight year old in the gradual process of developing a strong "backbone". I mentioned earlier Kate, who didn't want to learn the piano. Of course, parents have to be flexible and tolerant, but for Kate's parents to give way every time that Kate disliked something would have been a completely different matter. Kate had tried the piano; her mother had struggled to help her through her boredom and awkwardness by encouraging her, making her do her practice, describing the pleasures of music. In this case Kate's wish *not* to be like her elder siblings and *not* to fit into her mother's ideas was simply too strong. But at least she didn't give up before she started.

With some new enterprise it is often a help if parents

give free rein to their confidence that there really *is* satisfaction to be derived from it, and don't leave the child to make all the running and to take all the decisions. A fine balance has to be achieved: children need to be able to make choices, but they aren't yet equipped to make them all, or to make big ones. James could read very well by the time he was eight and a half. However, although he loved stories (and an eight year old still enjoys being read to at times) James was quite content to look at comics and television rather than story-books. His father and mother didn't want to push him because they were afraid of putting him off reading. They were a bit taken aback, however, to hear him say in a lordly way to his friends, "Books are boring! I hate reading!" He couldn't mean it? or could he? It wasn't as though, like many children of his age, James found reading so laborious that it couldn't be much fun. Did he need help to get down to it? His parents decided that the Summer holidays would be an ideal time to start James off on reading. They were going to a cottage that had no television. On the first evening James's mother read to him, as she still sometimes did. She started a new book. She said, "And tomorrow evening you can carry on by yourself." James made a face. He fully expected to be let off. But next evening his mother insisted. He could either read or lie straight down and go to sleep. After some sulky demurring, James reached out for the book. Each evening his mother persisted. By the second week of the holiday James was reading not only at bed-time. When they returned home his parents were determined it shouldn't stop, and they allowed time deliberately for bed-time reading.

Over this minor matter James had been helped by his parents' united determination. Their combined strength of purpose had made him feel unconsciously that it was possible to combat reluctance. They found a similar thing working when he moved to a school that had homework some evenings. There was an awful rumpus at times after the initial novelty had worn off, but his parents took it in turns, not to do his homework, but to sit with him while he did it. Funnily enough, that seemed to be sufficient to make him feel that he was getting moral support. James was getting the feeling that his parents knew he didn't always want to do some things: they could bear this knowledge and they didn't fall into a panic. They just stood firm. A child who does not have a parent who can persevere even in the knowledge that the child doesn't like something is a deprived child. All children need some grown ups in their lives who will give them space to choose (and to make mistakes) but who will also put up with their anger, resentment, sulkiness and will not be too frightened by it. This is how children grow up being able to manage their own feelings; they gradually become able to *know* that something makes them feel doubtful, cross, nervous or unwilling – and yet still have the strength to persevere and to carry on. They take in, internalise and become strong people.

When things go wrong: picking up the pieces

We have just been thinking about security and support. What happens when misfortune strikes? Major or minor crises will occur in the life of any eight year old, just as they will at eighteen or eighty. Are there any general principles about handling unhappy experiences?

Perhaps we could ask ourselves how anyone in the normal way recovers from bad experiences. First, we are dependent on our resources - the resources of trust, hopefulness and optimism which were first laid down in babyhood if we had ordinarily good enough care, and which are constantly developed, replenished and brought up to date by current good experiences. Second, with the resources at our command we start to work away on a bad experience. Consciously and unconsciously we think it over, puzzle away at it, try to understand it so that it becomes more bearable. Often it appears in dreams, either directly or in a fragmented or disguised form – a sign that we are working on it unconsciously, with that part of our mind which is below the surface. This is hard, because the essence of an unpleasant experience lies in the fact that it arouses unpleasant feelings – fear, disgust; a sense of being lonely, rejected, humiliated; perhaps feelings of envy, unsatisfied greed, jealousy, revenge. Thinking it over involves us in tackling these feelings, all of which and more are perfectly normal and universal. So we cannot hope to get away without encountering circumstances which inspire them.

The most frequent unpleasant experiences for children could well be family quarrels. Lydia, for example, was dreadfully thrown by the way in which her elder sisters, now teenagers, were prepared to have some fairly ruthless rows with their parents. It was impossible to shield Lydia from these; the atmosphere of discord was all-pervasive and no-one could fail to notice it. One of her elder sisters was doing well at school but was in head-on conflict with her parents about her boy-friend; the other was causing anxiety because of academic failure. From Lydia's point of view (these upsets had been boiling up since she was six or so) it seemed as though growing up meant growing up to be unpleasant. The father and mother who had seemed capable of resolving any difficulty (in her small-child's imagination) suddenly took a toss and were revealed as disagreeing with each other, unable to deal with recalcitrance, thoroughly worried. Lydia felt her whole world to be rocking around her – she was unable to see it as a passing phase, because she had no adult perspective to resort to. She was *inside* the family; the family was her world, and she felt thoroughly unsettled.

What does one do in circumstances like this? The worst thing for anyone is to feel alone with unhappiness. So it was a comfort to Lydia when her mother, seeing her burst into tears after witnessing a row, realised all at once how upset Lydia was getting. She took Lydia on her knee and tried to talk about things being difficult. Lydia needed only a little encouragement and, with hesitation at first but then more fluently, she began to say how she hated these rows, how nasty she thought her sisters were sometimes and how she wished it would all stop. Not all children come out with things easily, but it is a help to them simply to know that you have noticed something is wrong and that you take it seriously.

It is painful to be aware that one's child is unhappy and we all have some temptation to push away awareness of it. In another family there was serious discord between the parents. The husband was having an affair with another woman; the wife knew about this but felt quite unequipped to face single parenthood and hoped that for the children's sake the couple could stay together. Her husband sometimes wanted to stay, sometimes to go. They thought they were concealing all knowledge of this from the children, and they managed to keep up an undemonstrative civility in front of them. But though the children did not know the facts of what was wrong, something made its way into their minds. The elder child became depressed and had for the first time ever a poor school report: the second child started stealing little unimportant things: the youngest was horribly irritable and clingy. Hidden discord was working upon them as surely as open discord. There seems to be no substitute for the truth: not, of course, always the whole truth in the kind of detail that can only raise more anxiety than it settles. In this case it became clear that no matter how painful it might be, the only relief these children could have would be for the parents to acknowledge to them openly that they, the parents, were not getting on well together at present. This, of course, could only provide partial relief: the relief that comes from realising that you aren't imagining things. The truth of the matter was that the situation was a painful one and could not be resolved without some suffering. But this was better for the children than flat denial from the parents and claims that everything was fine.

In this case it was only too clear what was upsetting these children. In other cases it is by no means plain. If you think your child is unhappy, how do you investigate this? The most important thing is already achieved: you have noticed. You have received the distress signals. Children often communicate somewhat indirectly, by inspiring feelings in us as well as by directly telling us in words. Sometimes it is anxiety they inspire. By losing appetite, being unable to sleep, or in an infinite number of more subtle ways a child can cause his or her father or mother to feel, "What's the matter? If he doesn't eat he'll be ill! If she doesn't sleep she'll get overtired! Why can't he eat? Why can't she sleep? Is she ill?" These questions are the beginnings of an attempt to understand what is wrong. Sometimes the child doesn't know what is wrong and direct questionings soon become persecutory. "What's *wrong*, darling?" comes to invite the answer "Nothing!" or, "I don't know." Parents have to look around in all departments of a child's life for signs of strain. What's happening at school? What's happening between the parents? Is there something like illness, bereavement, unemployment somewhere in the family? We often do not know how much to worry. Should we have confidence that difficulties will pass? or do we need to take action? Seek professional advice? A book like this cannot start to answer those questions. A good rule, perhaps, is to take your time, think things over and delay action unless you are perfectly certain that you have identified the cause. In the sad family mentioned earlier, where the parents' marriage was under threat, there would have been no point in responding to the elder child's poor school report by blaming the school, thinking it didn't suit the child, and considering a new school.

There are occasions, of course, where vigorous action is the right remedy. Bullying may be one of these. But when the school has been alerted, when the teacher has been consulted, when the bully has been stopped, we still have to think, "Why was *this* child bullied?" There can be all sorts of complicated answers to this question. Children can be timid because they are afraid of their own aggression; so afraid that they dare not even stick up for themselves. Adrian, mentioned much earlier, told his father that he'd learnt what to do if somebody came along in a threatening way. "You've got to look a bit fierce," he said, "or they just go away and fetch their friends." Both bully and victim need our thoughtful attention. First the behaviour has to be stopped – no doubt about that. Then it has to be investigated and understood.

The successful negotiation of minor misfortunes results in the development of emotional muscle. Then, when larger difficulties strike a child is fitter to receive them. There will be difficulties which parents cannot solve or remove. Illness, hospitalisation and operations, divorce, death in the family – all these major unhappinesses can strike a child as they can adults. The best we can do for children in these circumstances is not to neglect them, not to leave them alone with the task of coming to grips with pain or loss. Plenty of opportunities should be given to children to talk about these big problems. Of course, it has to be done sensitively, discreetly and taking the child's own pace as a guide. Who doesn't remember some grown ups being intrusive and embarrassing? Equally, we may all have memories of someone who seemed to us as a child a nice grown-up, one to be turned to, who was sympathetic and receptive.

Friends and relationships

Finally, I should like to say something about the development of friendships, which by this age involve many a child in real rounded relationships, relationships that inspire thoughtfulness, consideration and concern for the other as well as mutual activities and rivalries or quarrels. In the usual way children learn about a full range of feelings at home, in the context of a family who can be relied upon to tolerate it. It doesn't matter whether the family is very small (just a mother or just a father) or whether there are many brothers and sisters and extra people. By the age of eight a gradual process of translating all the lessons learnt in human relationships to friendships outside the family is clearly observable. It starts much earlier, of course, but tiny children can't be relied upon to stay in command of their feelings and earlier friendships need an adult eye on them much of the time.

Peter was a little older than James, his neighbour. They were going together on a day activity course. School had broken up, and both their mothers worked. James was nervous about this. The boys were fond of each other and despite his nervousness James was looking forward to the games and activities and trusting in Peter's company to help him. On the Monday morning Peter wasn't well, and his mother said he couldn't go. She went down to telephone James's mother, and when she got back she found Peter close to tears. He said he was worrying about James - poor James, would he be all right?

A small example like this shows how Peter had been able to feel for James, to think what things would be like from James's point of view, even to put that first. Yet, of course, this did not preclude the two boys being quite different on other occasions. Peter was capable of preferring his class-mates, boys of exactly the same age, to James. It was a healthy sign that neither boy treated the other as though he were made of china and would break at a small blow. Most children shift and vary in their friendships. It is only when extremes are reached that we really need to worry. The child who has no friends, or who has no permanent friends, is a child who cannot be experiencing himself as likeable. Problems of fitting in, problems of sharing, problems of seeing the other person's point of view – none of these are solved by an eight year old, but they should be in the process of being tackled.

Conclusion

An eight year old is into the middle years of childhood. The passion and intimacy of babyhood and the early years are past. There is some sort of lull before puberty arrives, and after that the years of adolescence with their quest for a child's adult identity. That identity will not easily be found unless these middle years can have something of solidity and consolidation about them.

FURTHER READING

On Learning to Read: the child's fascination with meaning, Bruno Bettelheim, Thames & Hudson, London, 1982
Children's Minds, Margaret Donaldson, Fontana, 1978
Parenting Threads: caring for children when couples part, National Stepfamily Association, 1992
The Emotional Experience of Learning and Teaching, Isca Salzberger-Wittenberg, Gianna Henry & Elsie Osborne, Routledge & Kegan Paul, London, 1983

HELPFUL ORGANISATIONS

Exploring Parenthood, Latimer Education Centre, 194 Freston Road, London W10 6TT. (National Advice Line for parents: 081-960-1678, 10.00 – 4.0 p.m. Monday to Friday)
National Stepfamily Association, 72 Willesden Lane, London NW6 7TA. (071-372-0844)
National Children's Bureau, 8 Wakley Street, London, EC1V 7QW.
Advisory Centre for Education, 18 Victoria Park Square, London, E2 9PB. (081-980-4596)

UNDERSTANDING YOUR CHILD

ORDER FORM FOR TITLES IN THIS SERIES

Send to: Rosendale Press Ltd., Premier House
10 Greycoat Place, London SW1P 1SB

Price per volume: £4.75 inc. post & packing

Understanding Your Baby by Lisa Miller ..... copies
Understanding Your 1 Year Old by Deborah Steiner ..... copies
Understanding Your 2 Year Old by Susan Reid ..... copies
Understanding Your 3 Year Old by Judith Trowell ..... copies
Understanding Your 4 Year Old by Lisa Miller ..... copies
Understanding Your 5 Year Old by Lesley Holditch ..... copies

Price per volume: £5.65 inc. post & packing

Understanding Your 6 Year Old by Deborah Steiner ..... copies
Understanding Your 7 Year Old by Elsie Osborne ..... copies
Understanding Your 8 Year Old by Lisa Miller ..... copies
Understanding Your 9 Year Old by Dora Lush ..... copies
Understanding Your 10 Year Old by Jonathan Bradley ..... copies
Understanding Your 11 Year Old by Eileen Orford ..... copies
Understanding Your Handicapped Child by Valerie Sinason .... copies

Total amount enclosed: £. . . . .
Name . . . .
Address . . . .
. . . . Post code . . . .